CW01390575

NAIL ART

SKETCHBOOK

WITH PROMPTS

Almond Shaped Nails

Belongs To:

_____

Welcome to Your New Nail Art Design Journal and Sketchbook!

This nail art journal was designed for the nail art enthusiast at all levels, from novice to professional.

I have included weekly prompts to help get the creative juices flowing. There are 52 prompts so you have a whole year of ideas to choose from.

Fill in the included blank color wheel with the coloring tool of your choice. Use your completed color wheel to pick color palettes and test how colors will look together.

Suggestions for how to use your new journal:

1. Jot down design ideas
2. Practice designs
3. Swatch polishes and refer back to swatches
4. Swatch topcoats over new or favorite polishes
5. Swatch sheer over opaque polishes
6. Test color combinations
7. If you use peel-off base coats, you can tape your peeled off designs in your journal!

Use **#apolishedreaderprompts** to share your interpretations of each prompt or just to share your use of this sketchbook with the nail art community!

A full list of the prompts can be found on the last page.

I hope you enjoy using your new design journal!

Thank you!
DJ

apolishedreader@gmail.com
@apolishedreader

COLOR WHEEL

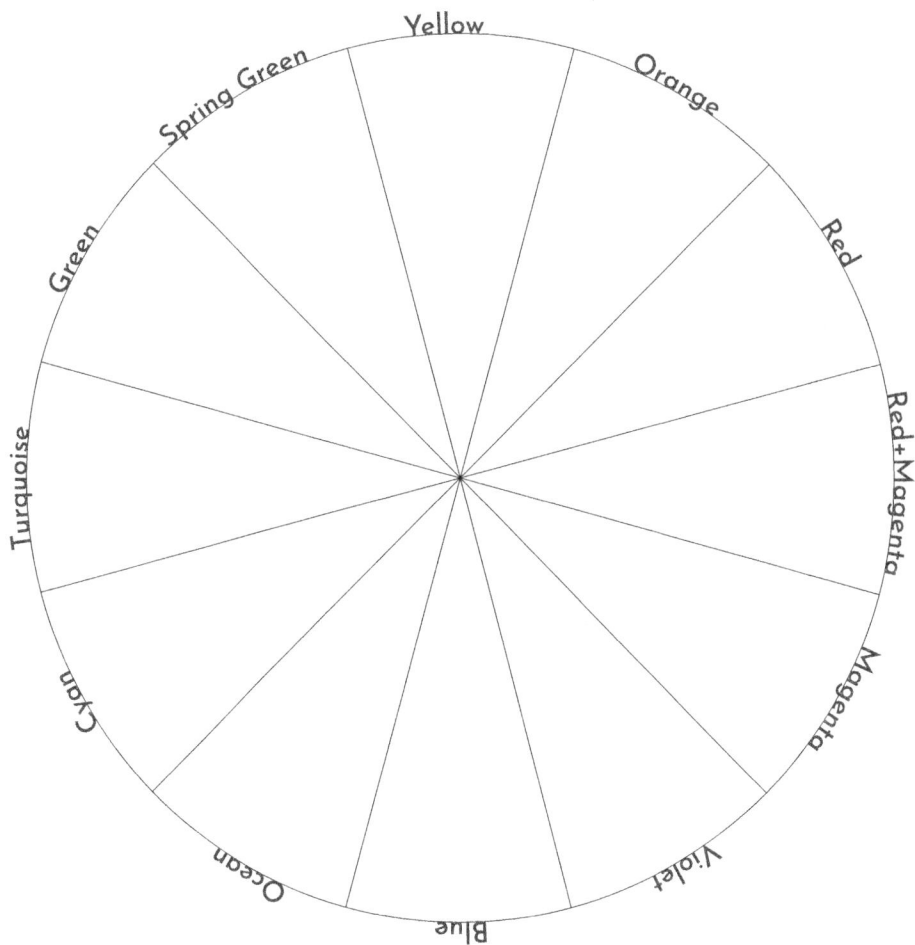

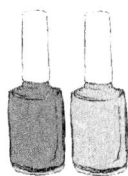

SWATCHES

NAME: NAME: NAME:

BRAND: BRAND: BRAND:

NAME: NAME: NAME:

BRAND: BRAND: BRAND:

NAME: NAME: NAME:

BRAND: BRAND: BRAND:

NAME: NAME: NAME:

BRAND: BRAND: BRAND:

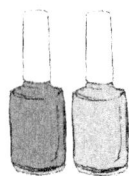

SWATCHES

NAME:

BRAND:

NAME:

BRAND:

NAME:

BRAND:

NAME:

BRAND:

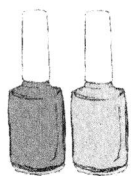

SWATCHES

NAME:

NAME:

NAME:

BRAND:

BRAND:

BRAND:

NAME:

NAME:

NAME:

BRAND:

BRAND:

BRAND:

NAME:

NAME:

NAME:

BRAND:

BRAND:

BRAND:

NAME:

NAME:

NAME:

BRAND:

BRAND:

BRAND:

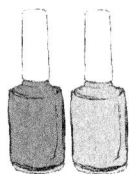

SWATCHES

NAME:

NAME:

NAME:

BRAND:

BRAND:

BRAND:

NAME:

NAME:

NAME:

BRAND:

BRAND:

BRAND:

NAME:

NAME:

NAME:

BRAND:

BRAND:

BRAND:

NAME:

NAME:

NAME:

BRAND:

BRAND:

BRAND:

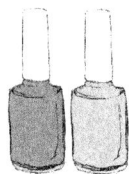

SWATCHES

NAME: NAME: NAME:

BRAND: BRAND: BRAND:

NAME: NAME: NAME:

BRAND: BRAND: BRAND:

NAME: NAME: NAME:

BRAND: BRAND: BRAND:

NAME: NAME: NAME:

BRAND: BRAND: BRAND:

Weekly Prompt

GOLD

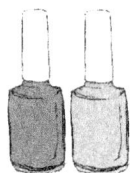

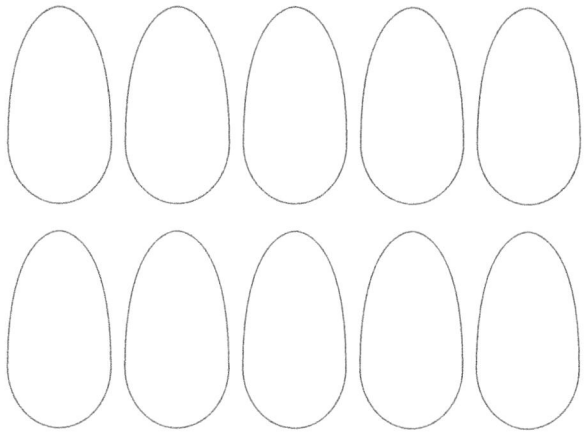

IDEAS / PALETTE

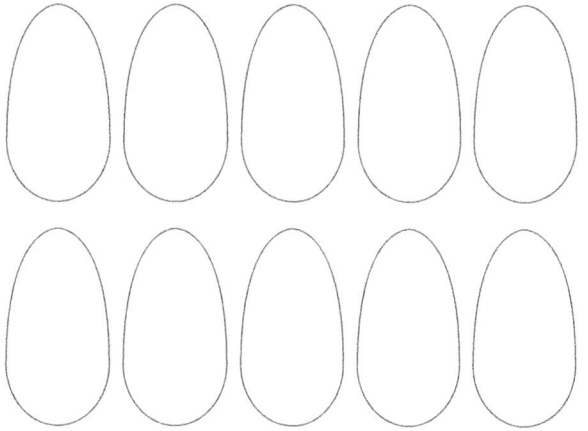

IDEAS / PALETTE

IDEAS / PALETTE

Weekly Prompt

PIZZA

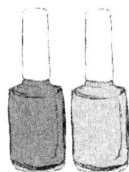

_____

_____

_____

_____

_____

_____

_____

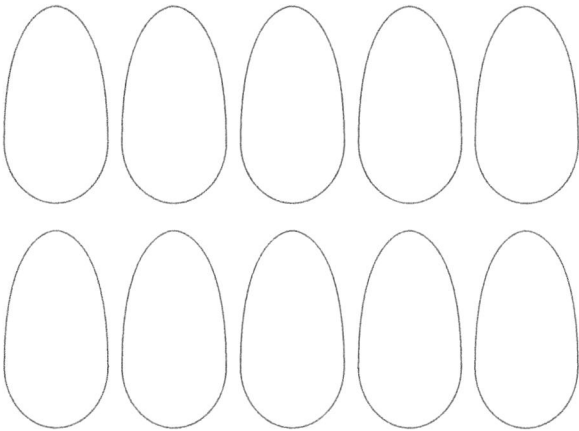

IDEAS / PALETTE

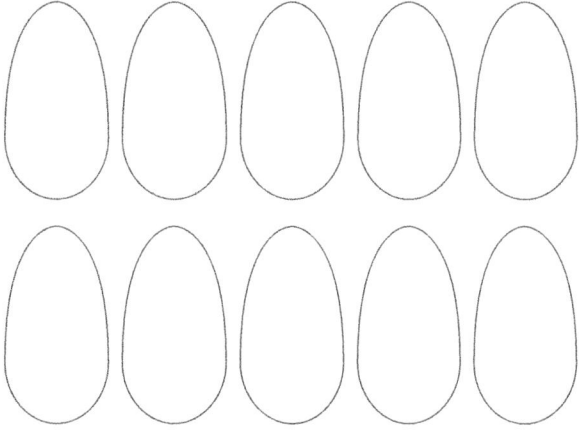

_____

_____

_____

_____

_____

_____

_____

IDEAS / PALETTE

Weekly Prompt

SUNRISE

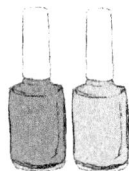

_____

_____

_____

_____

_____

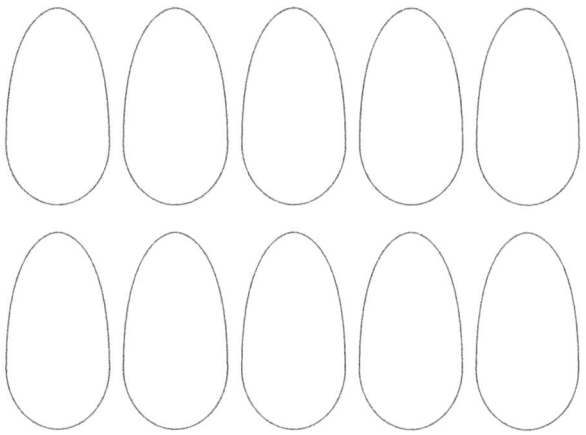

IDEAS / PALETTE

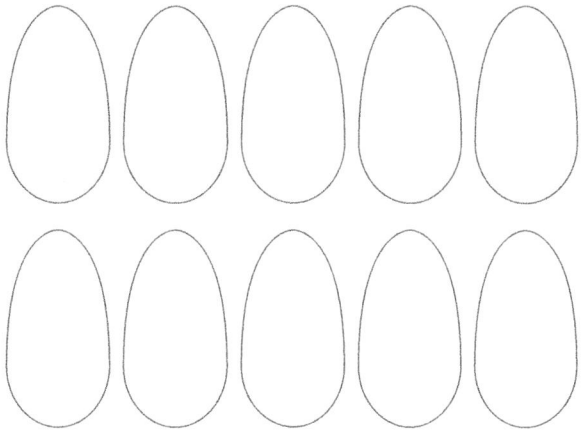

_____

_____

_____

_____

_____

IDEAS / PALETTE

Weekly Prompt

BLUE BIRD

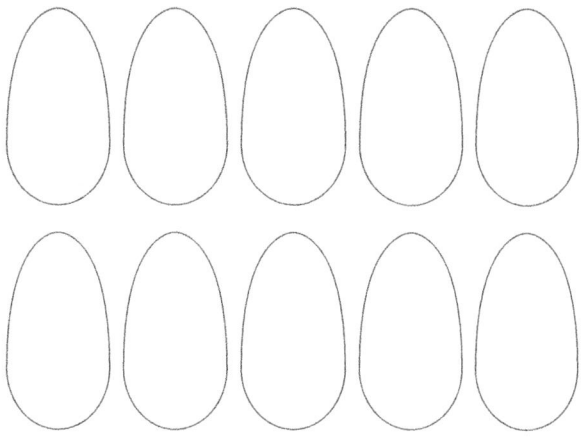

IDEAS / PALETTE

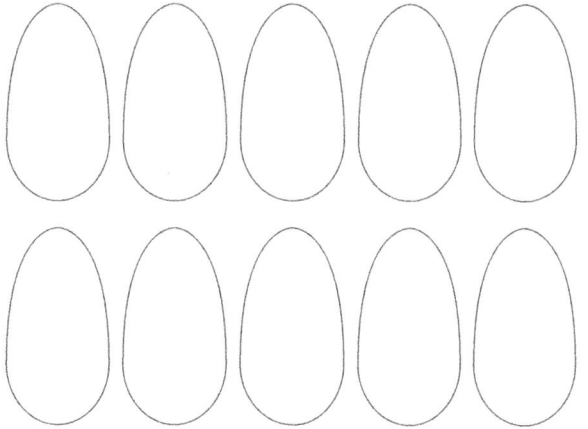

IDEAS / PALETTE

Weekly Prompt

SUSHI

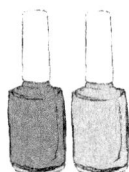

_____
_____
_____
_____
_____
_____

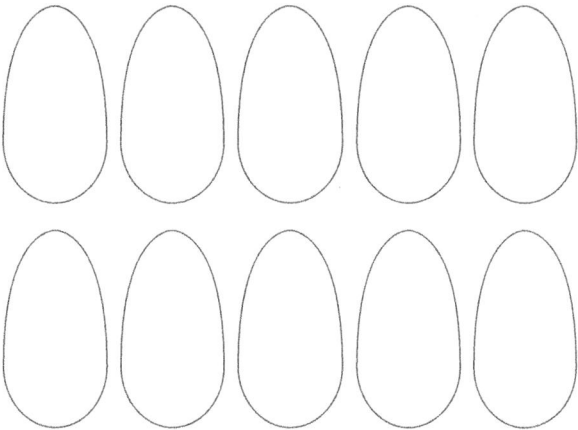

IDEAS / PALETTE

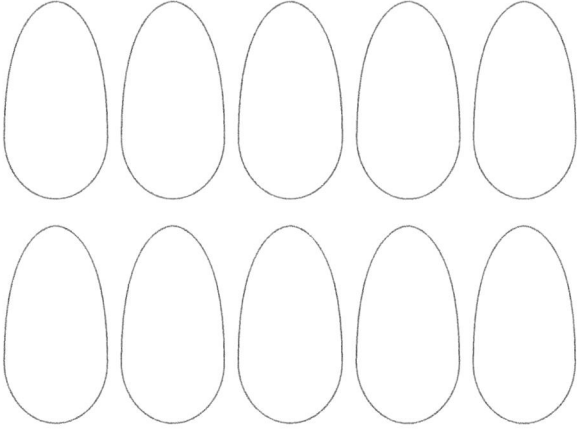

_____
_____
_____
_____
_____
_____

IDEAS / PALETTE

Weekly Prompt

HEARTS

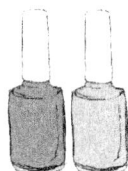

_____

_____

_____

_____

_____

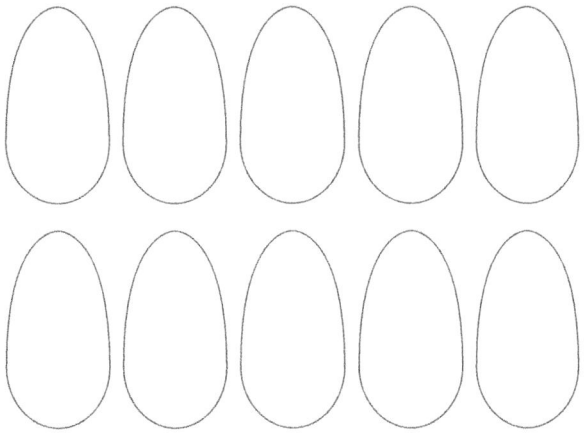

IDEAS / PALETTE

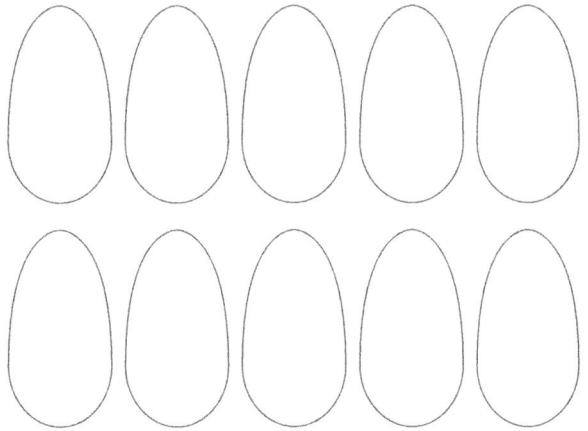

_____

_____

_____

_____

_____

IDEAS / PALETTE

Weekly Prompt

CHOCOLATE

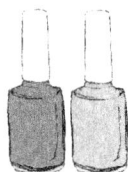

_____

_____

_____

_____

_____

_____

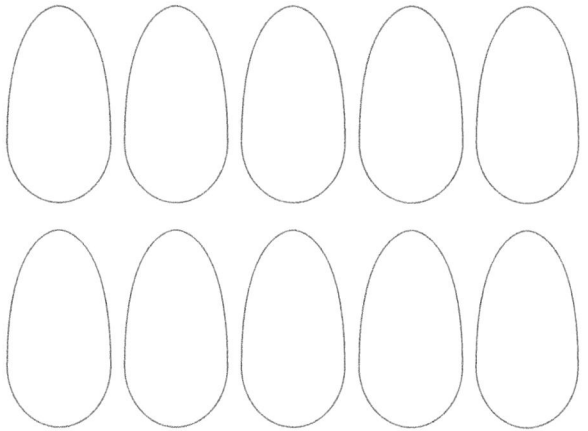

IDEAS / PALETTE

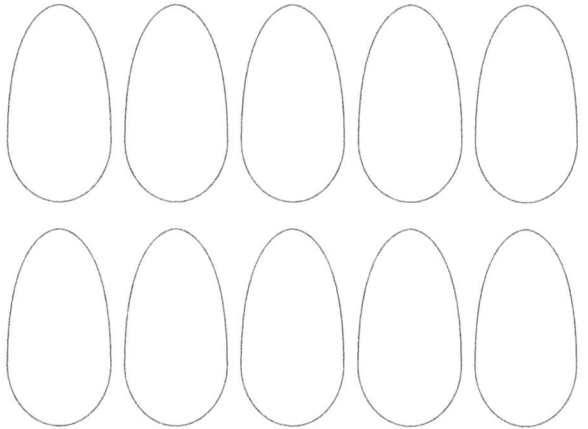

_____

_____

_____

_____

_____

_____

IDEAS / PALETTE

Weekly Prompt
GEOMETRIC SHAPES

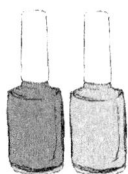

_____

_____

_____

_____

_____

_____

_____

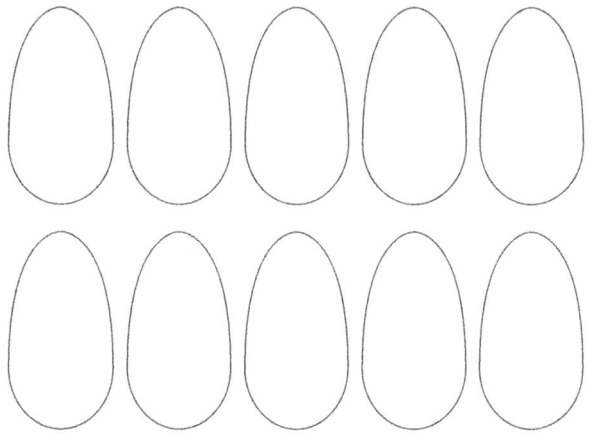

IDEAS / PALETTE

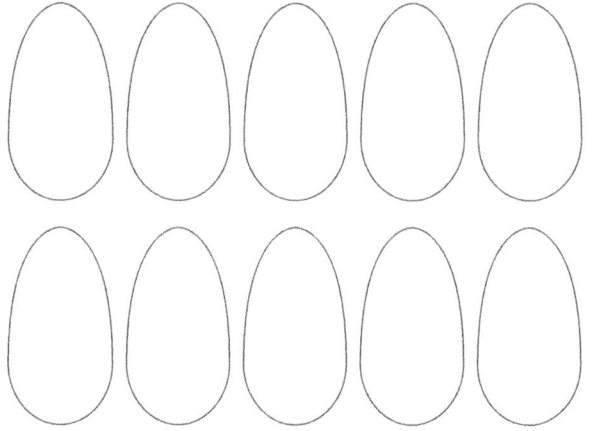

_____

_____

_____

_____

_____

_____

_____

IDEAS / PALETTE

Weekly Prompt

CAMERAS

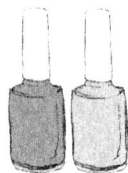

_____

_____

_____

_____

_____

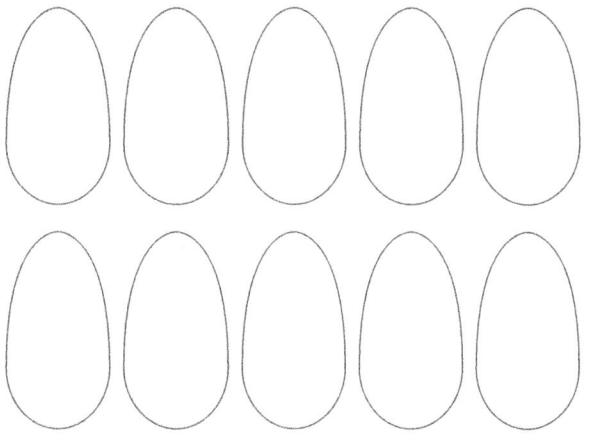

IDEAS / PALETTE

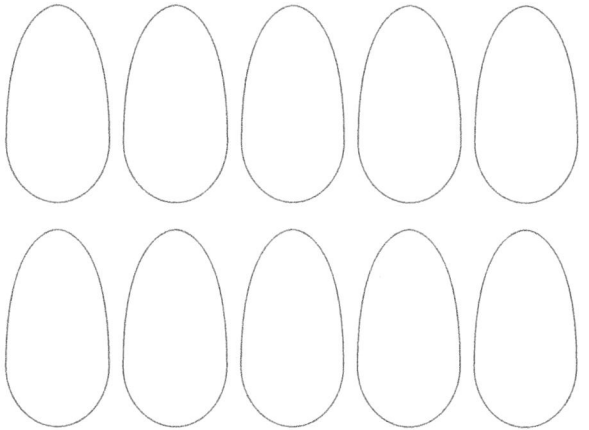

_____

_____

_____

_____

_____

IDEAS / PALETTE

Weekly Prompt

BOOKS

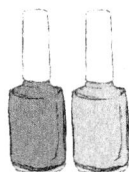

_____

_____

_____

_____

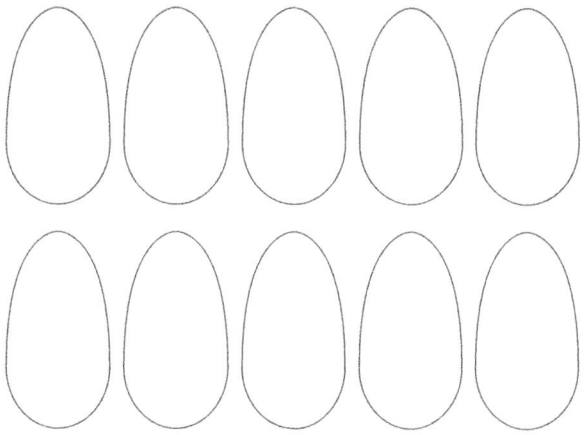

IDEAS / PALETTE

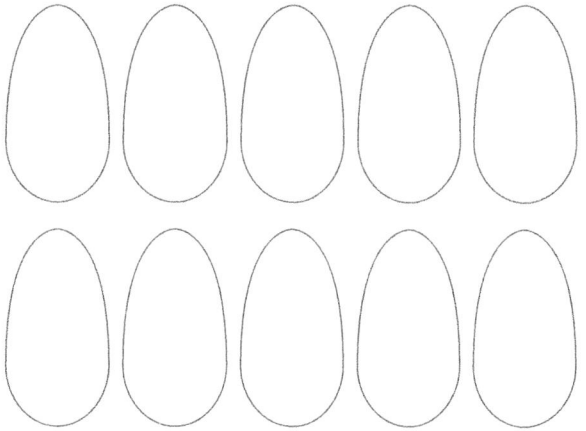

_____

_____

_____

_____

IDEAS / PALETTE

Weekly Prompt

LUCKY

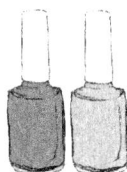

_____

_____

_____

_____

_____

_____

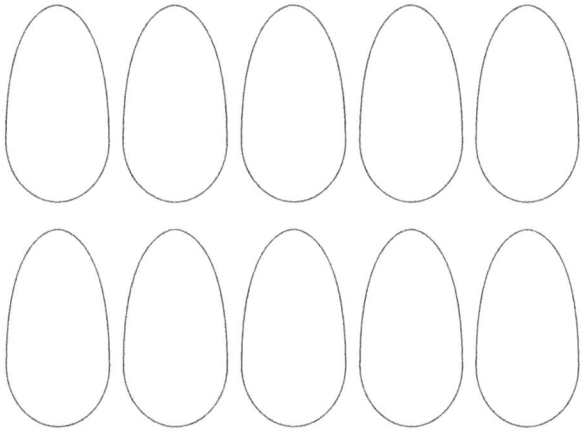

IDEAS / PALETTE

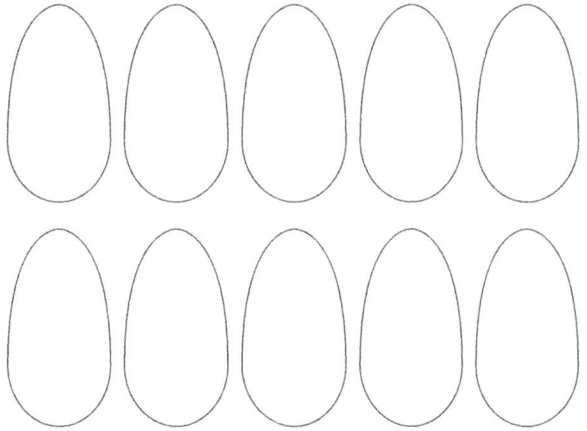

_____

_____

_____

_____

_____

IDEAS / PALETTE

Weekly Prompt

STRAWBERRIES

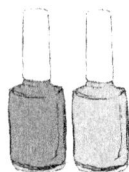

_____

_____

_____

_____

_____

_____

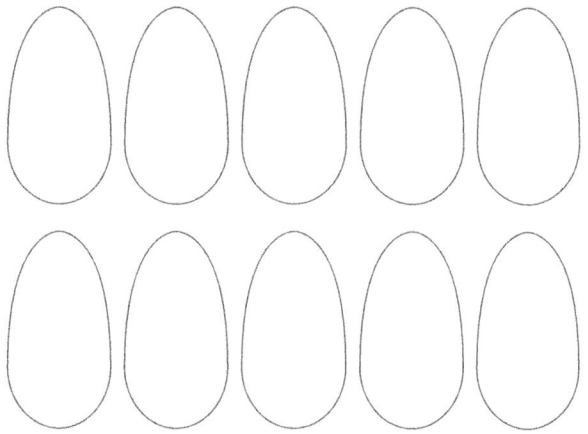

IDEAS / PALETTE

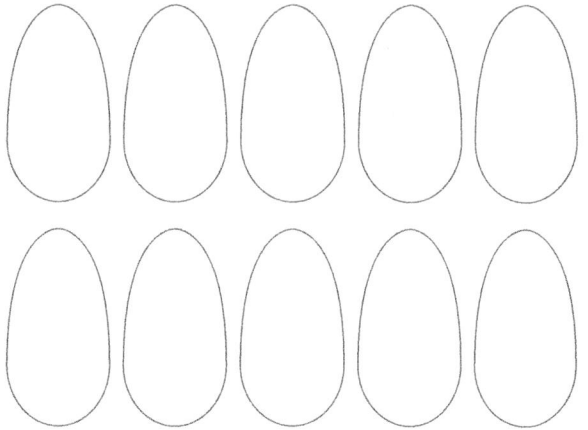

_____

_____

_____

_____

_____

_____

IDEAS / PALETTE

Weekly Prompt

CHICKENS

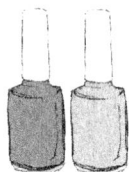

_____

_____

_____

_____

_____

_____

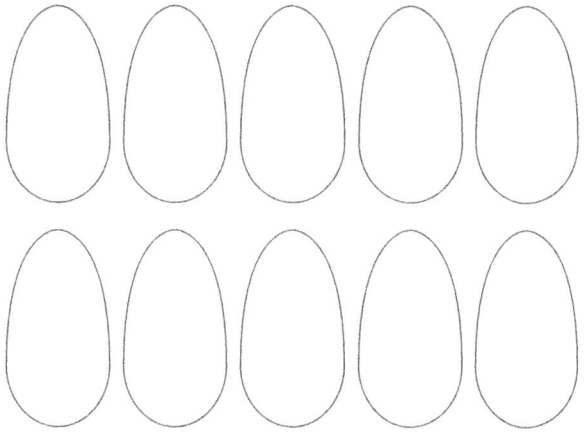

IDEAS / PALETTE

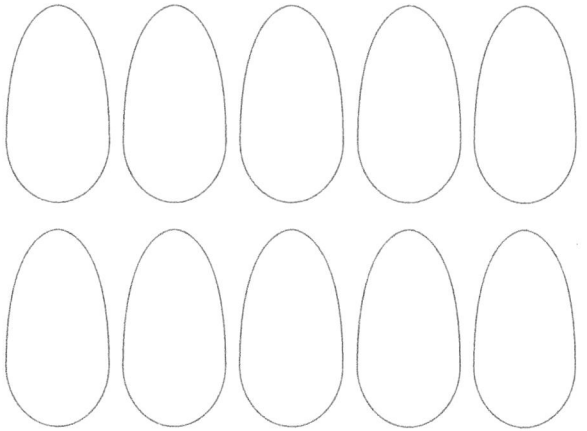

_____

_____

_____

_____

_____

_____

IDEAS / PALETTE

Weekly Prompt

PASTEL

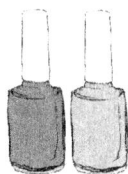

_____

_____

_____

_____

_____

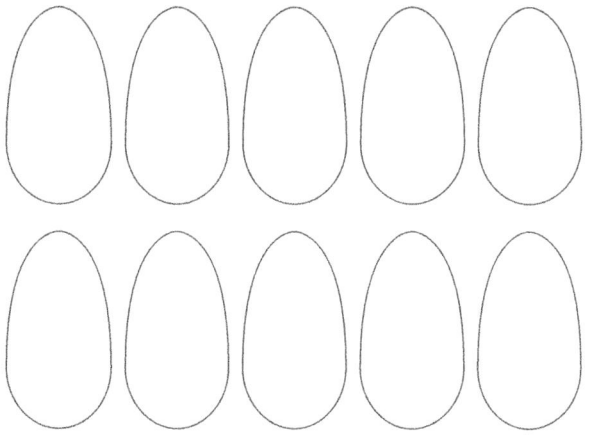

IDEAS / PALETTE

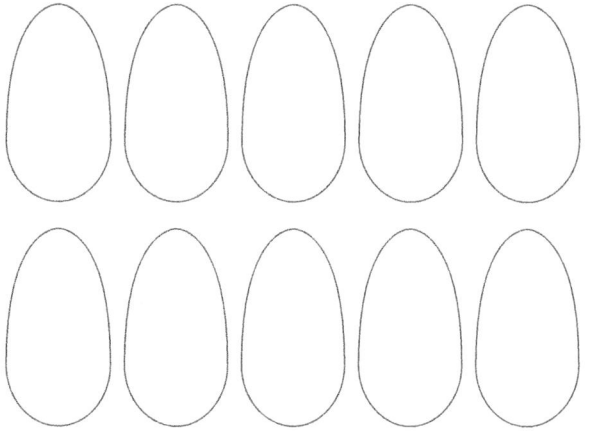

_____

_____

_____

_____

_____

IDEAS / PALETTE

Weekly Prompt

UMBRELLAS

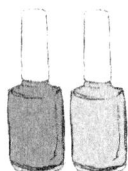

_____

_____

_____

_____

_____

_____

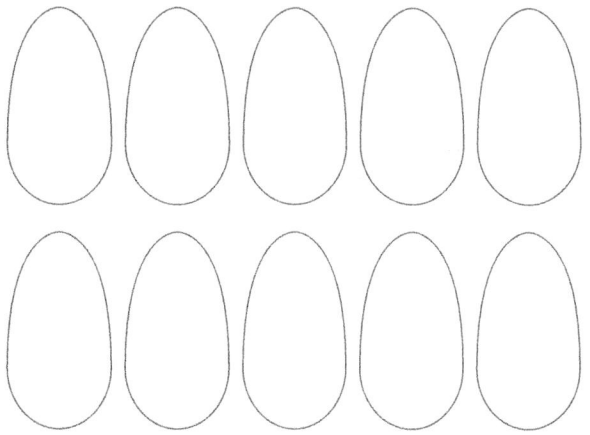

IDEAS / PALETTE

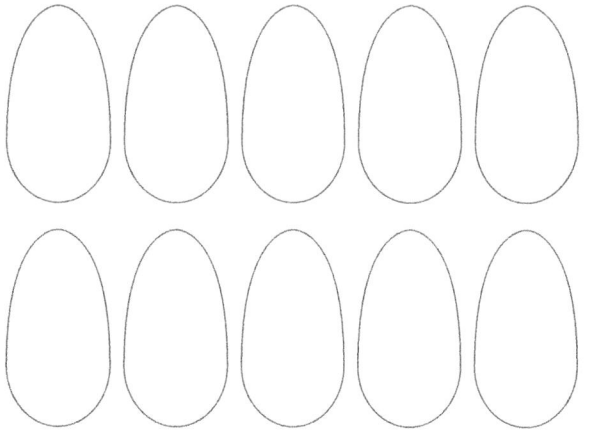

_____

_____

_____

_____

_____

_____

IDEAS / PALETTE

Weekly Prompt

GALAXY

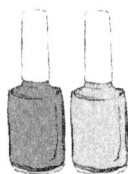

_____

_____

_____

_____

_____

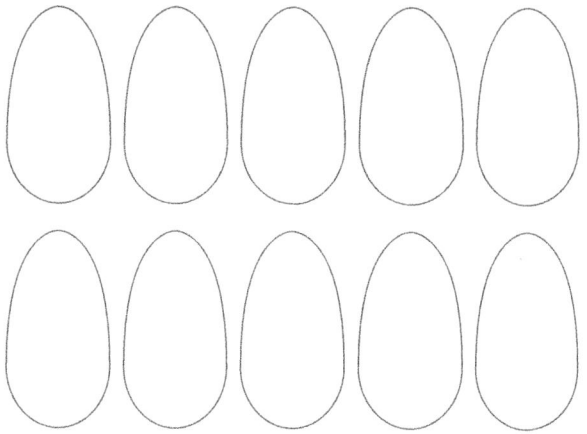

IDEAS / PALETTE

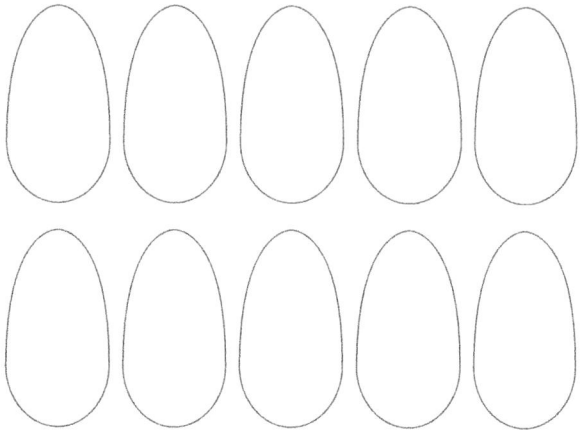

_____

_____

_____

_____

_____

IDEAS / PALETTE

Weekly Prompt

NEGATIVE SPACE

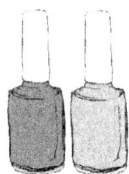

_____

_____

_____

_____

_____

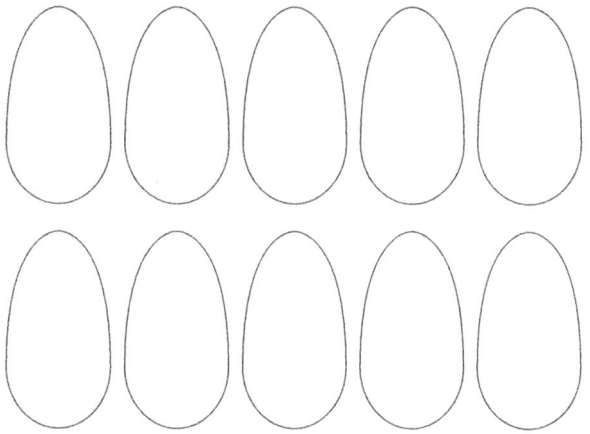

IDEAS / PALETTE

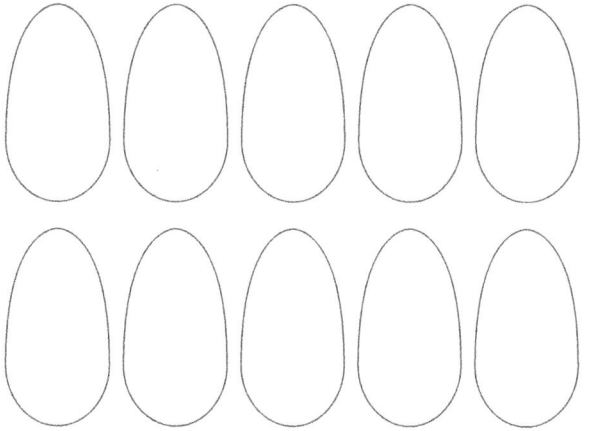

_____

_____

_____

_____

_____

IDEAS / PALETTE

Weekly Prompt

MARGARITAS

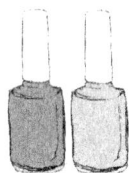

_____

_____

_____

_____

_____

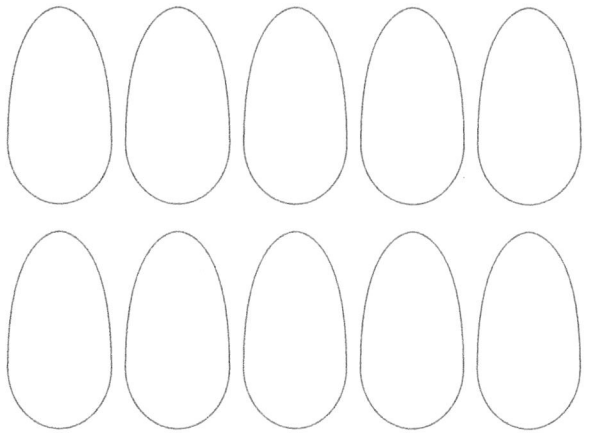

IDEAS / PALETTE

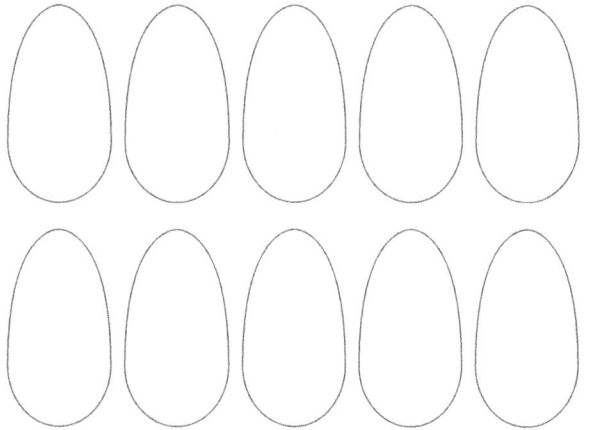

_____

_____

_____

_____

_____

IDEAS / PALETTE

Weekly Prompt

MERMAIDS

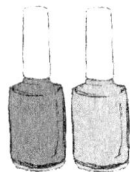

_____

_____

_____

_____

_____

_____

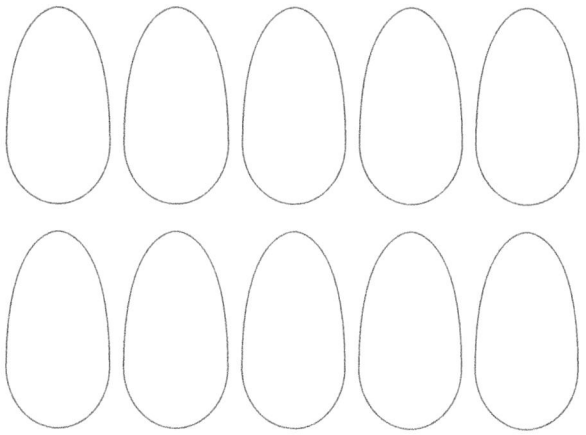

IDEAS / PALETTE

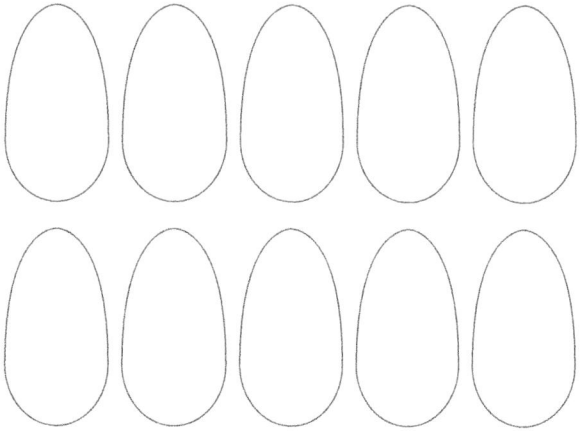

_____

_____

_____

_____

_____

_____

IDEAS / PALETTE

Weekly Prompt

LIGHTNING

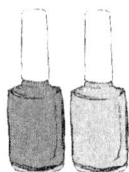

_____

_____

_____

_____

_____

_____

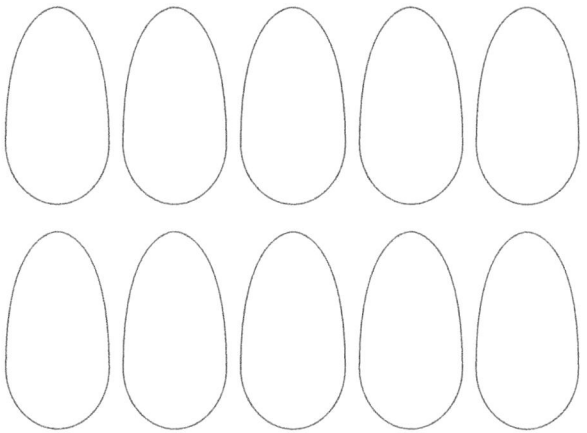

IDEAS / PALETTE

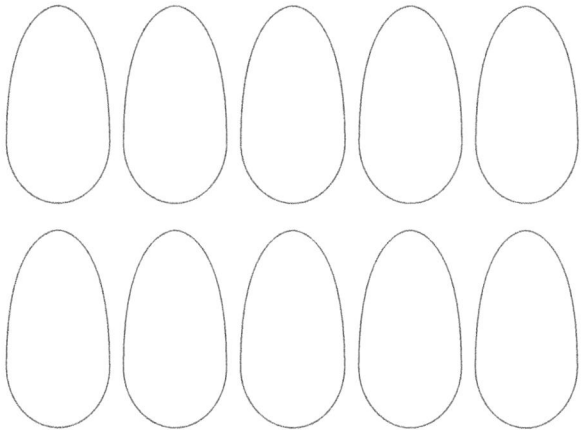

_____

_____

_____

_____

_____

IDEAS / PALETTE

Weekly Prompt

PINEAPPLES

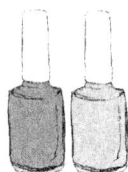

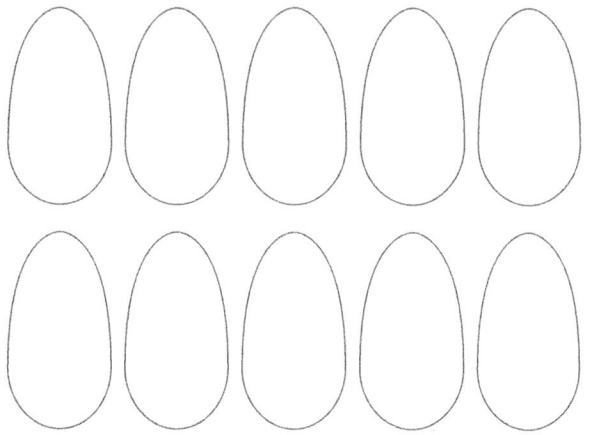

IDEAS / PALETTE

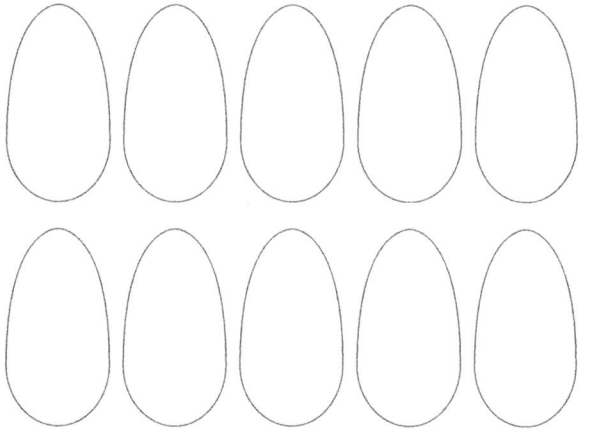

IDEAS / PALETTE

Weekly Prompt

RAINBOW

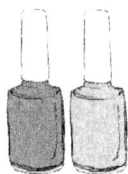

_____

_____

_____

_____

_____

_____

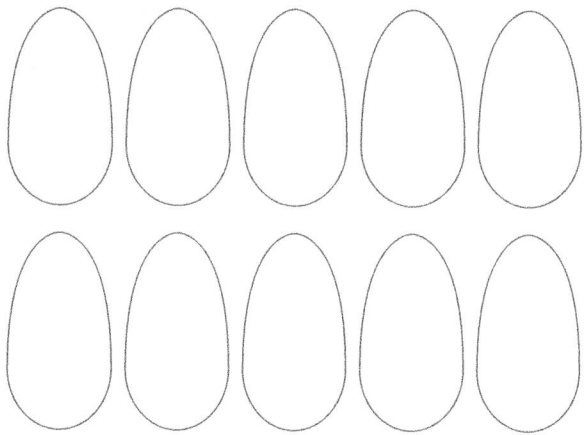

IDEAS / PALETTE

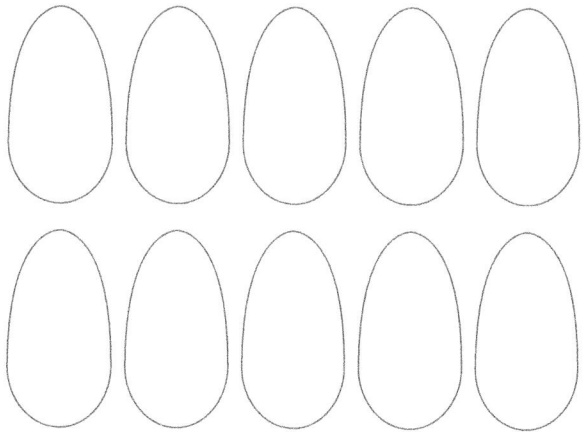

_____

_____

_____

_____

_____

_____

IDEAS / PALETTE

Weekly Prompt

BEACH

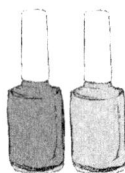

_____

_____

_____

_____

_____

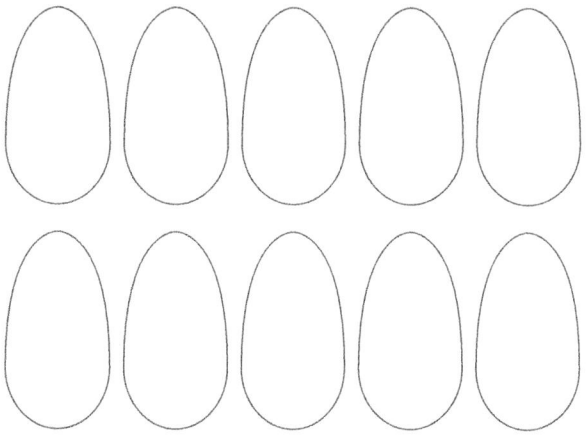

IDEAS / PALETTE

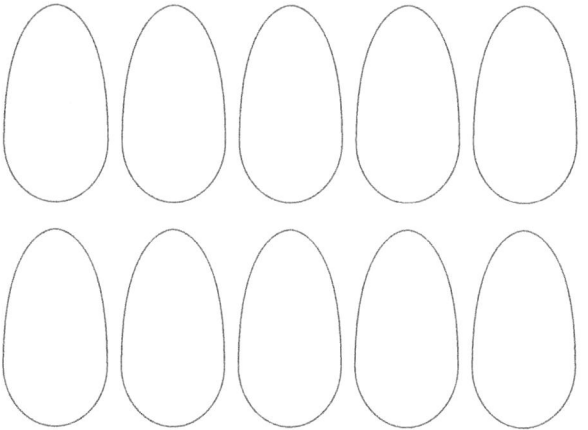

_____

_____

_____

_____

_____

IDEAS / PALETTE

Weekly Prompt

PLANETS

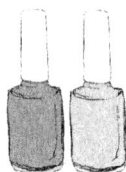

_____

_____

_____

_____

_____

_____

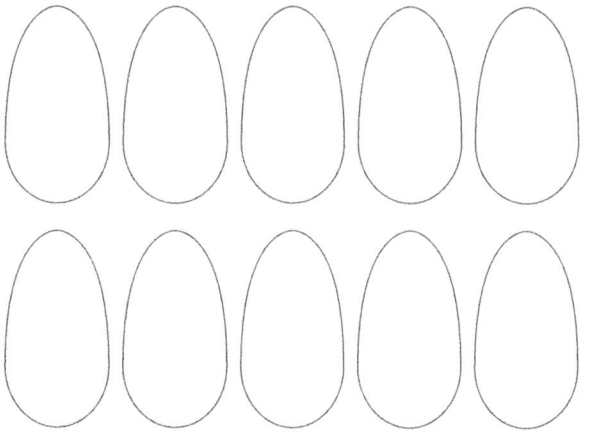

IDEAS / PALETTE

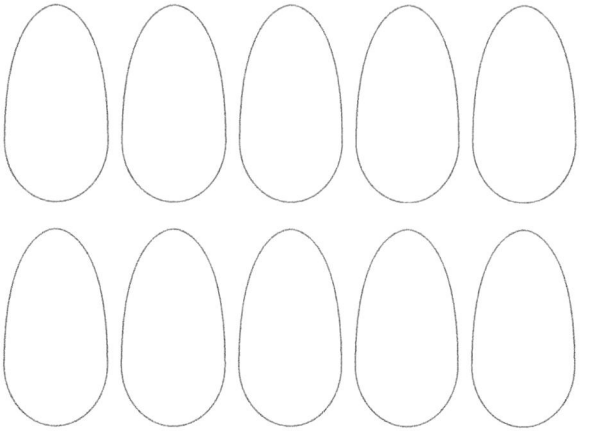

_____

_____

_____

_____

_____

_____

IDEAS / PALETTE

Weekly Prompt

CACTUS

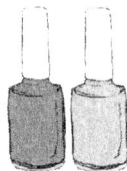

_____

_____

_____

_____

_____

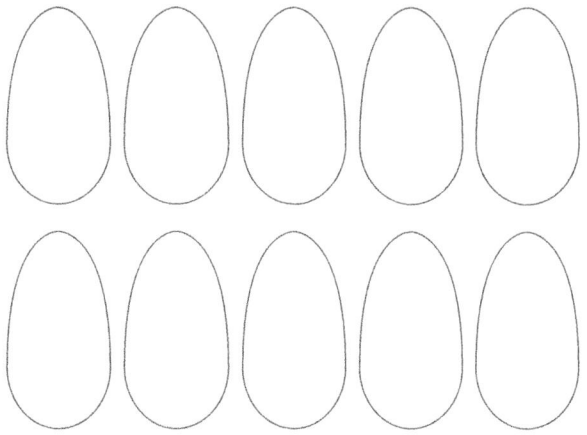

IDEAS / PALETTE

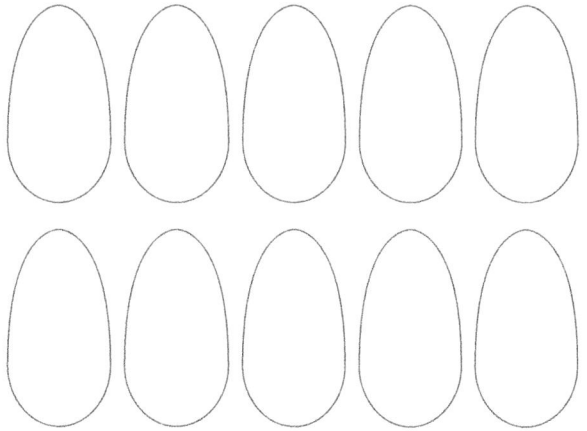

_____

_____

_____

_____

_____

IDEAS / PALETTE

Weekly Prompt

OCEAN

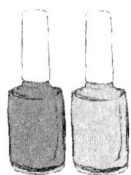

_____

_____

_____

_____

_____

_____

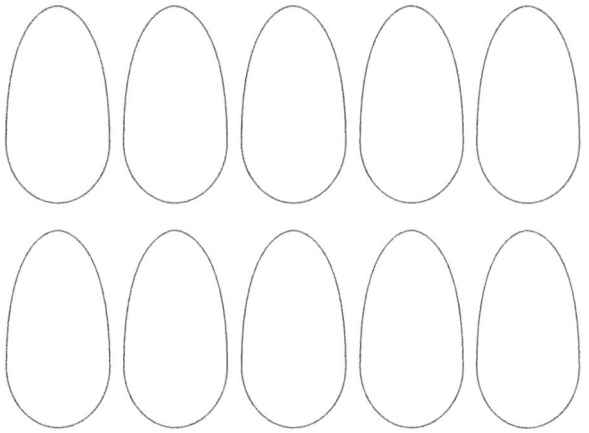

IDEAS / PALETTE

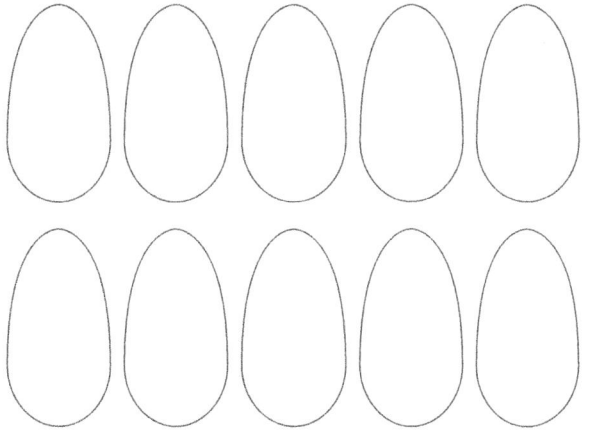

_____

_____

_____

_____

_____

_____

IDEAS / PALETTE

Weekly Prompt

FIREWORKS

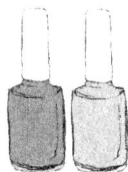

_____

_____

_____

_____

_____

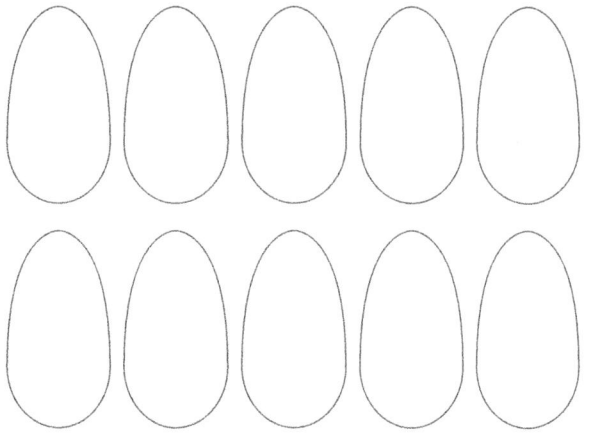

IDEAS / PALETTE

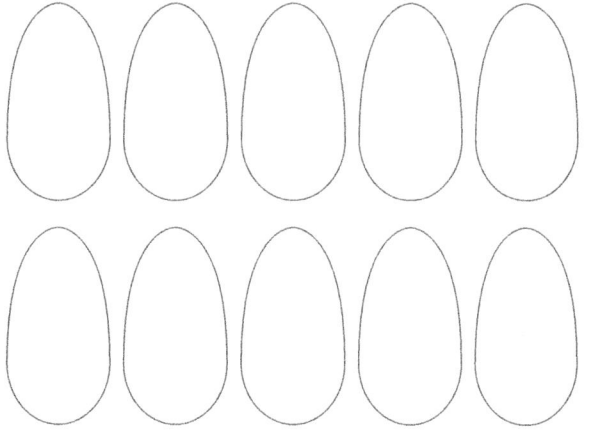

_____

_____

_____

_____

IDEAS / PALETTE

Weekly Prompt

DOGS

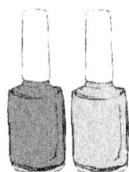

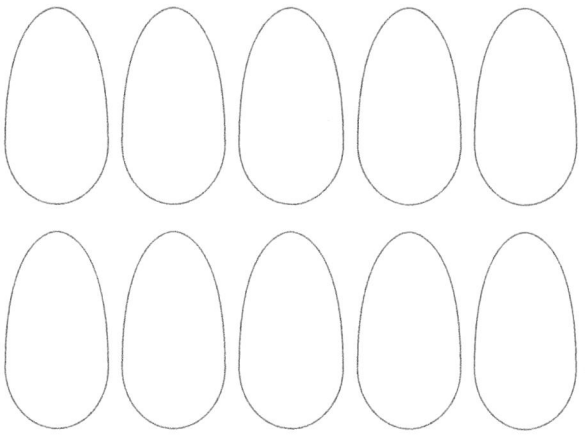

IDEAS / PALETTE

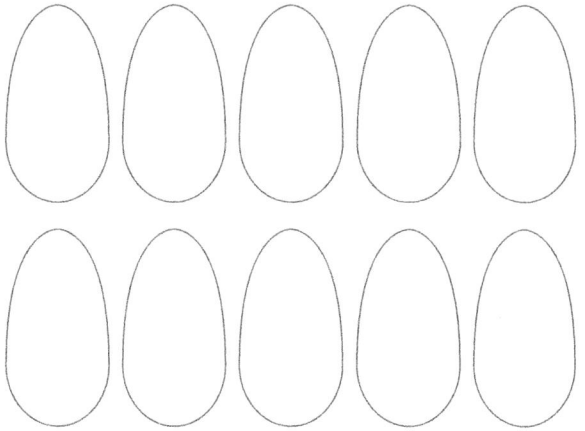

IDEAS / PALETTE

Weekly Prompt

ICE CREAM

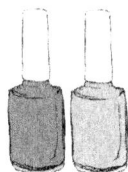

_____

_____

_____

_____

_____

_____

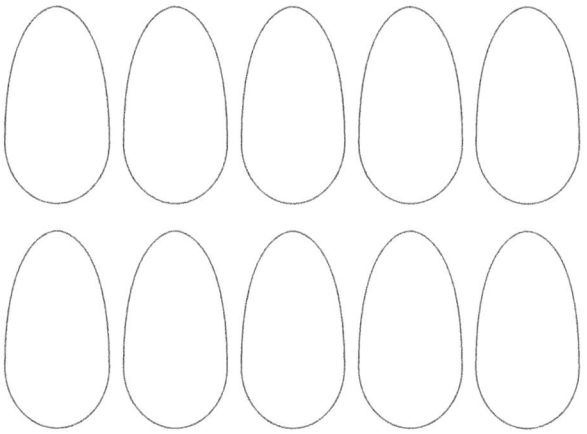

IDEAS / PALETTE

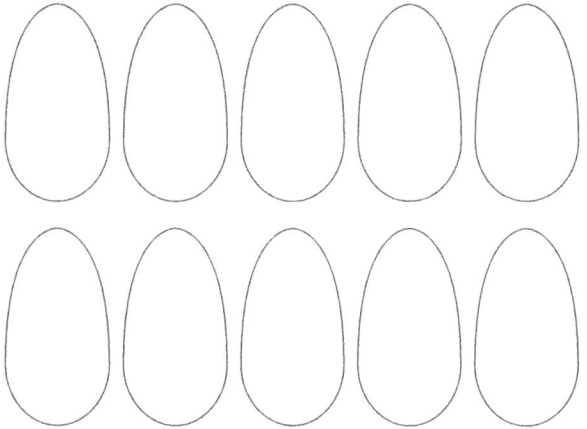

_____

_____

_____

_____

_____

_____

IDEAS / PALETTE

Weekly Prompt

SEA SHELLS

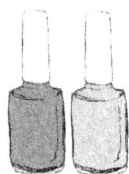

_____

_____

_____

_____

_____

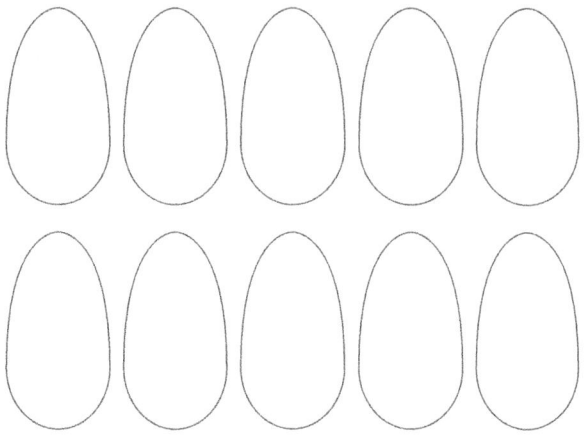

IDEAS / PALETTE

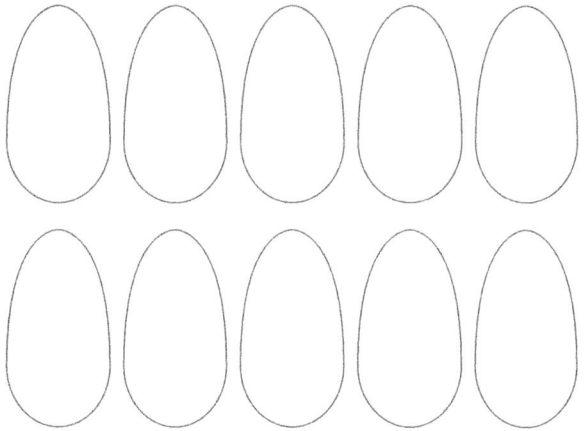

_____

_____

_____

_____

_____

IDEAS / PALETTE

Weekly Prompt

CAMOUFLAGE

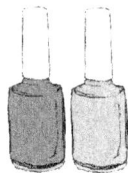

_____

_____

_____

_____

_____

_____

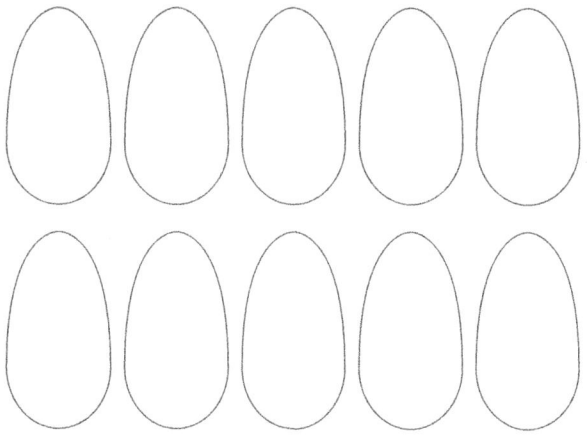

IDEAS / PALETTE

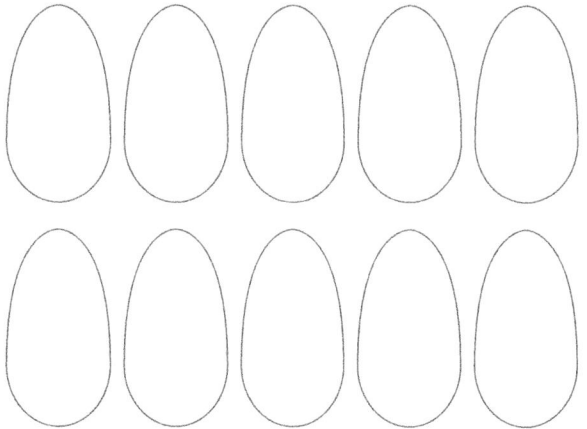

_____

_____

_____

_____

_____

_____

IDEAS / PALETTE

Weekly Prompt

ROSES

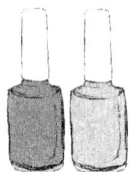

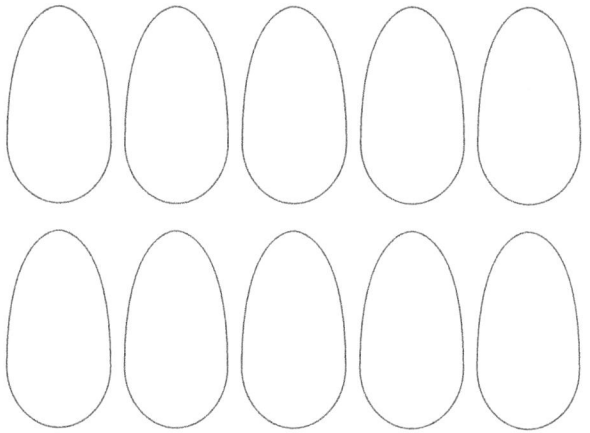

IDEAS / PALETTE

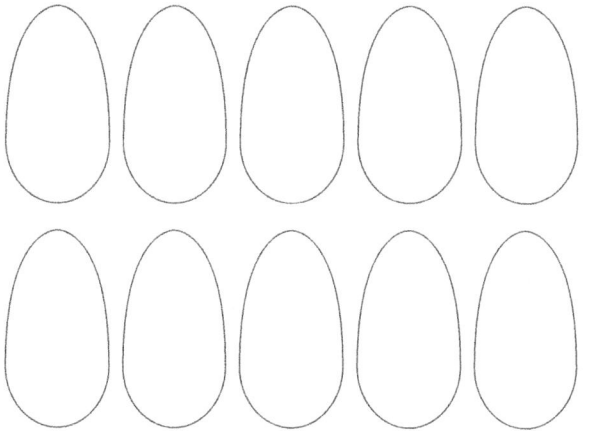

IDEAS / PALETTE

Weekly Prompt

BACKPACKS

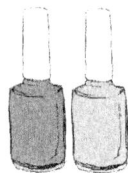

_____

_____

_____

_____

_____

_____

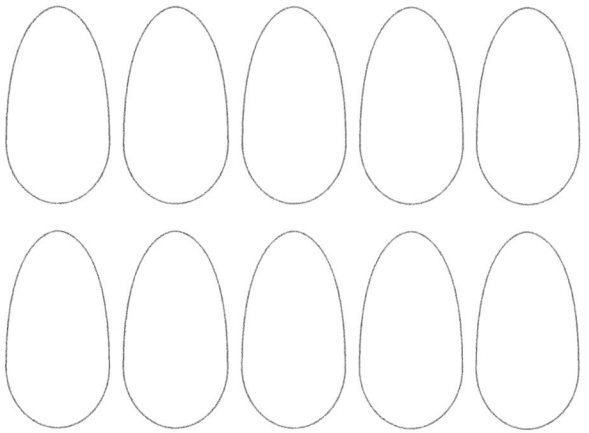

IDEAS / PALETTE

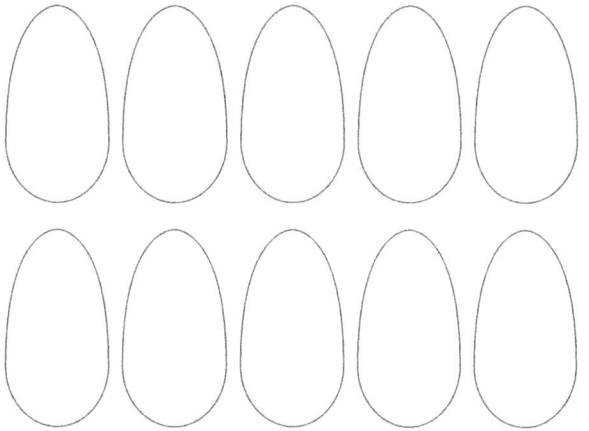

_____

_____

_____

_____

_____

_____

IDEAS / PALETTE

Weekly Prompt

SUNSET

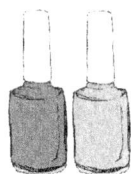

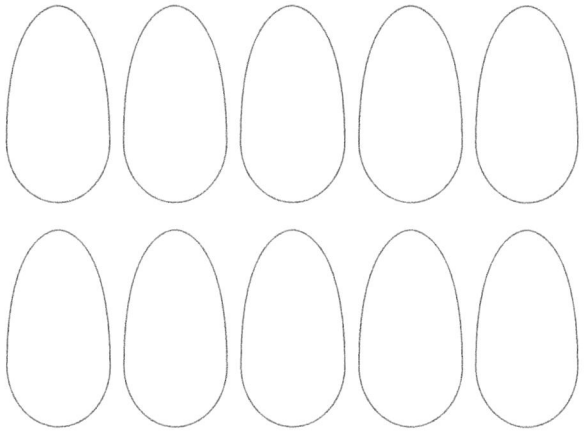

IDEAS / PALETTE

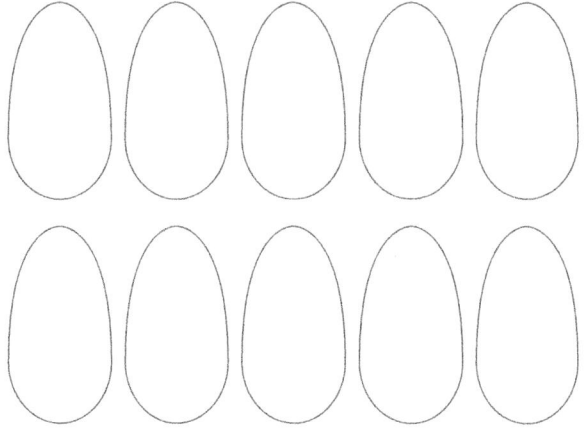

IDEAS / PALETTE

Weekly Prompt

WATERMELON

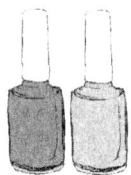

_____

_____

_____

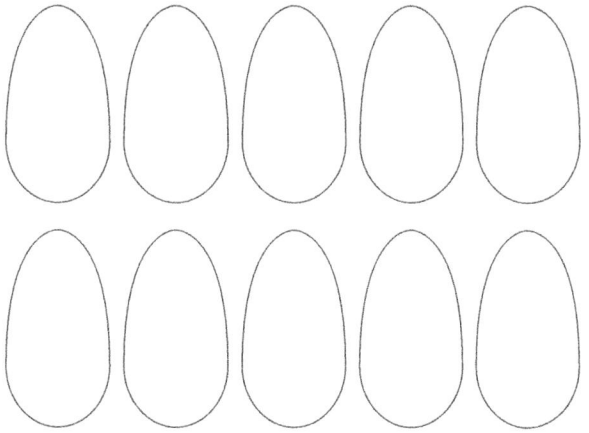

IDEAS / PALETTE

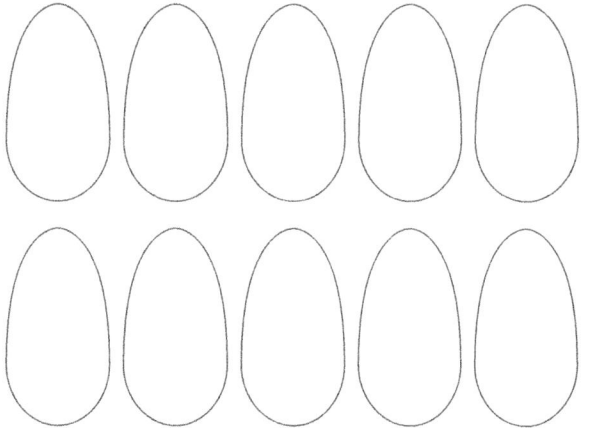

_____

_____

_____

IDEAS / PALETTE

Weekly Prompt

ABSTRACT ART

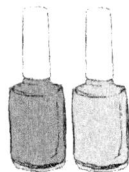

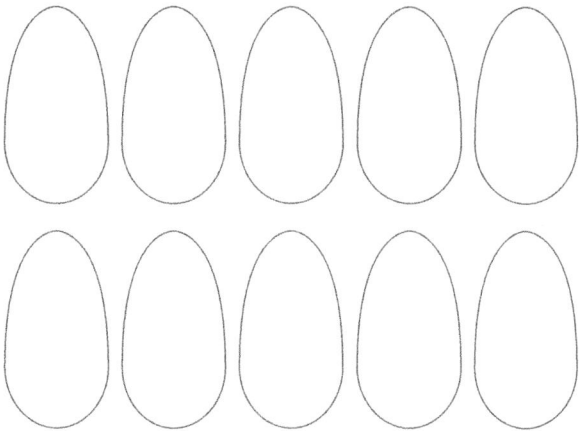

IDEAS / PALETTE

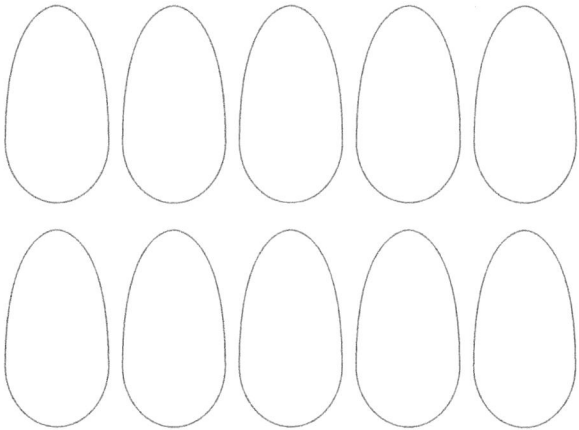

IDEAS / PALETTE

Weekly Prompt

CATS

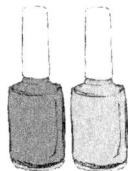

_____
_____
_____
_____
_____
_____

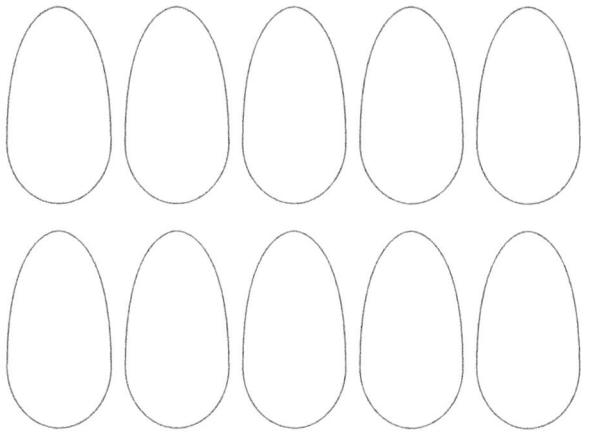

IDEAS / PALETTE

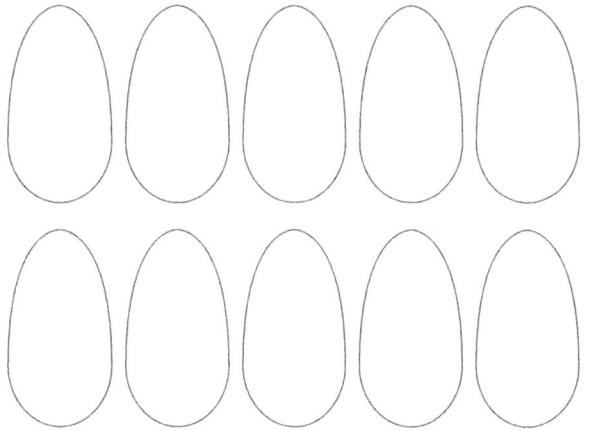

_____
_____
_____
_____
_____
_____

IDEAS / PALETTE

Weekly Prompt

PAISLEY

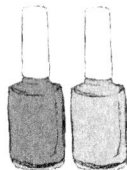

_____

_____

_____

_____

_____

_____

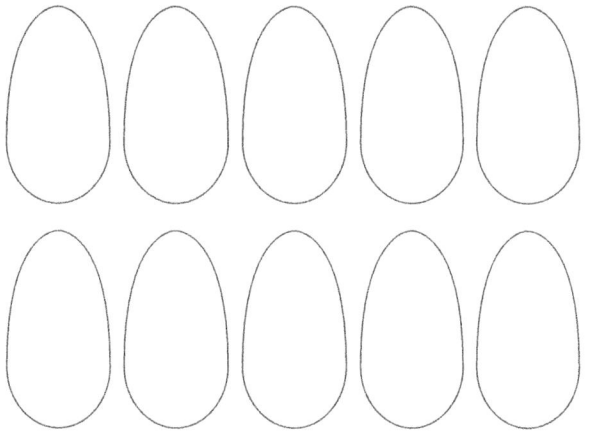

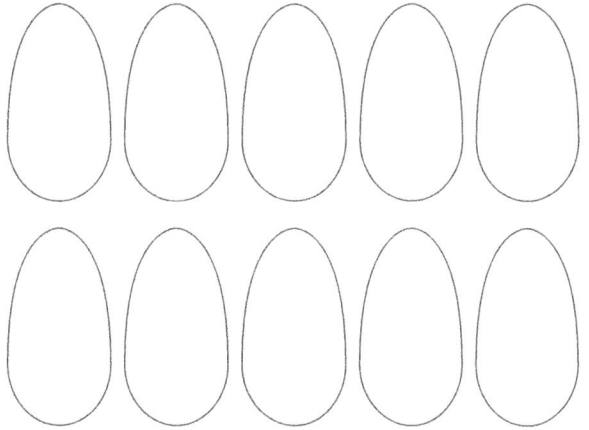

_____

_____

_____

_____

_____

_____

Weekly Prompt

COFFEE

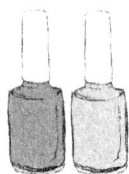

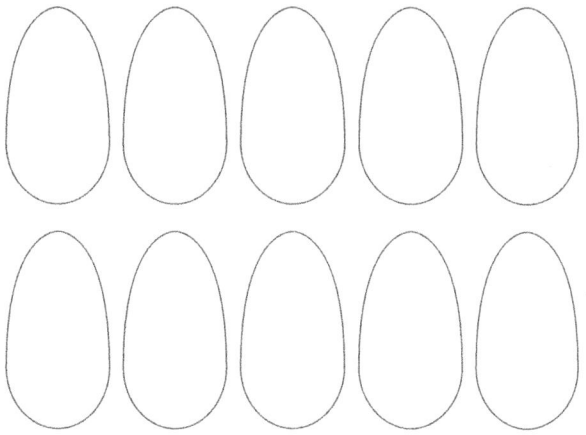

IDEAS / PALETTE

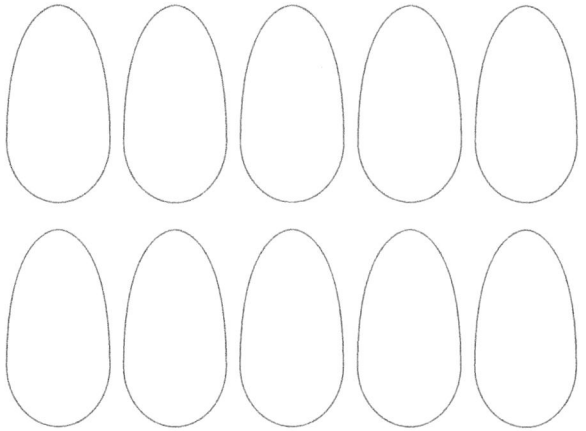

IDEAS / PALETTE

Weekly Prompt

SNAKES

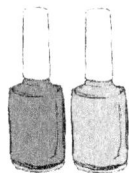

_____

_____

_____

_____

_____

_____

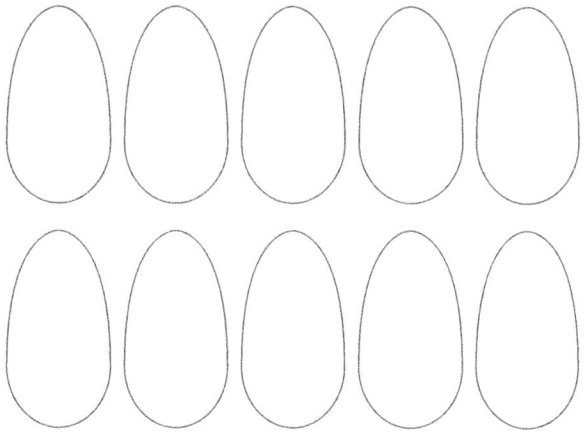

IDEAS / PALETTE

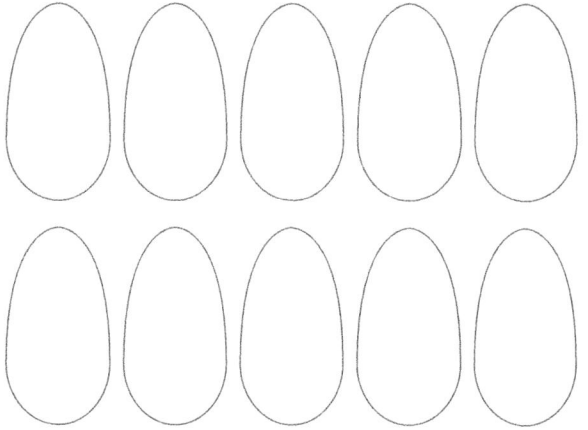

_____

_____

_____

_____

_____

_____

IDEAS / PALETTE

Weekly Prompt

FOREST

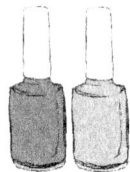

———————————
———————————
———————————
———————————
———————————
———————————

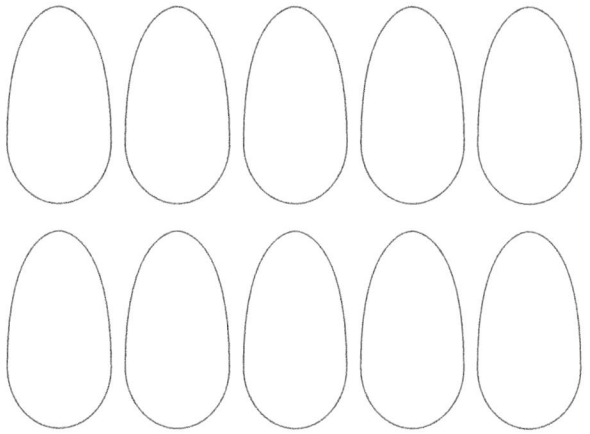

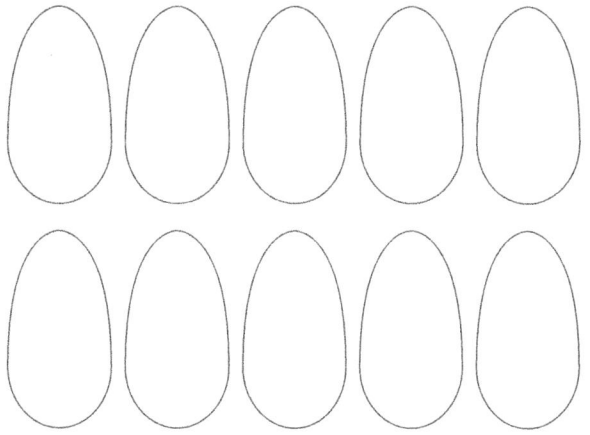

IDEAS / PALETTE

———————————
———————————
———————————
———————————
———————————
———————————

IDEAS / PALETTE

Weekly Prompt

VAMPIRE

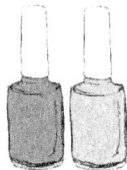

_____
_____
_____
_____
_____
_____

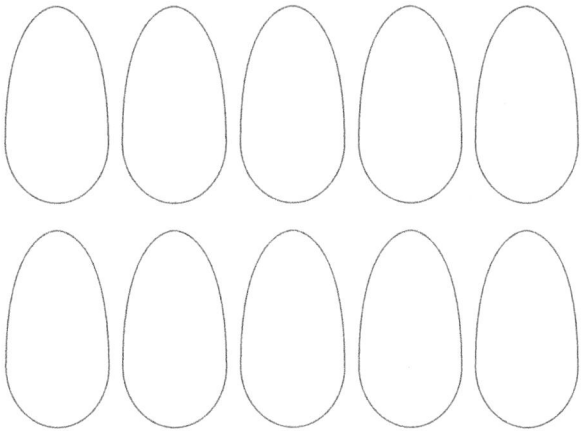

IDEAS / PALETTE

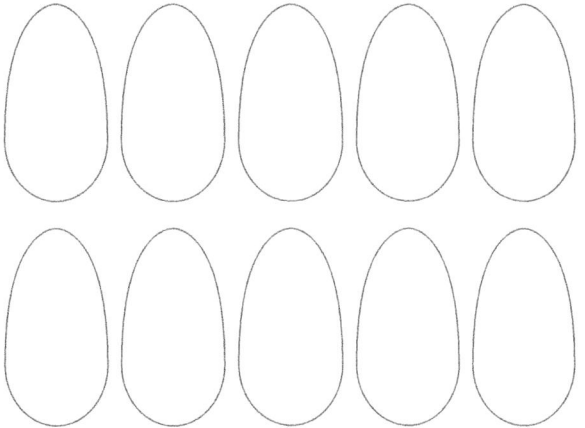

_____
_____
_____
_____
_____
_____

IDEAS / PALETTE

Weekly Prompt

CANDY CORN

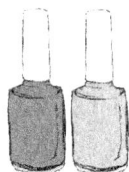

_____

_____

_____

_____

_____

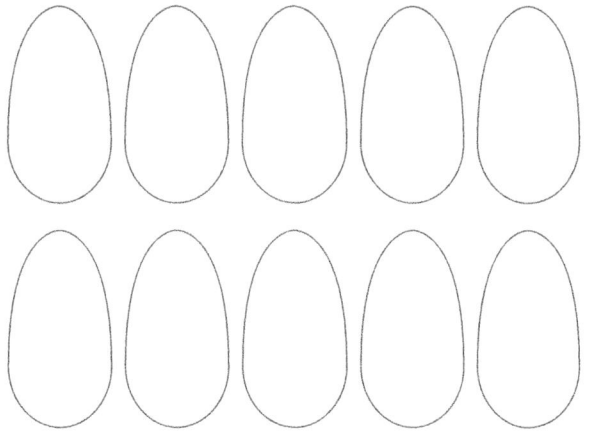

IDEAS / PALETTE

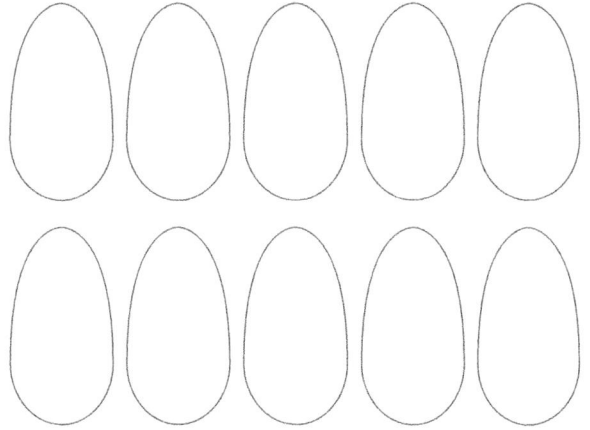

_____

_____

_____

_____

_____

IDEAS / PALETTE

Weekly Prompt

INK SPLATTER

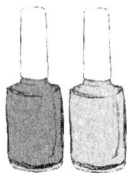

_____
_____
_____
_____
_____
_____

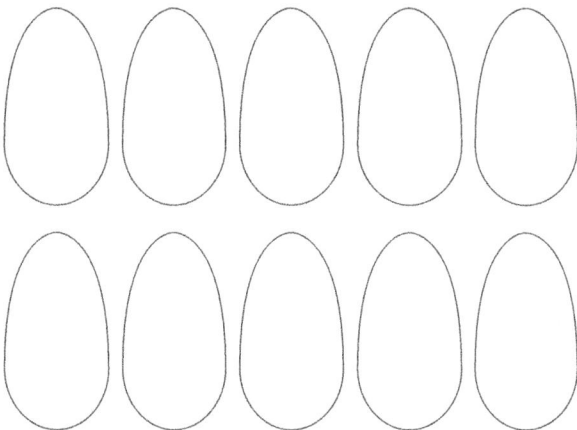

IDEAS / PALETTE

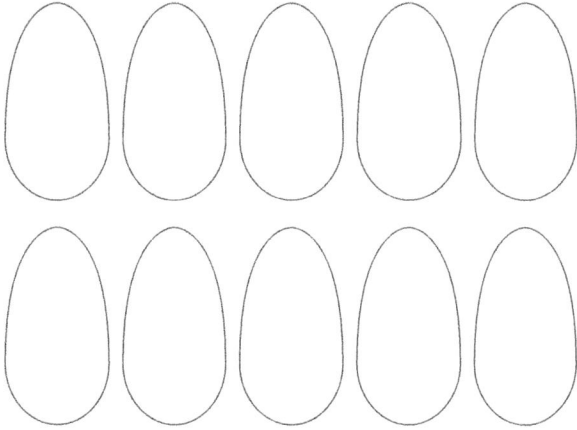

_____
_____
_____
_____
_____
_____

IDEAS / PALETTE

Weekly Prompt

CABLE KNIT

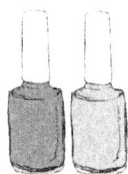

_____

_____

_____

_____

_____

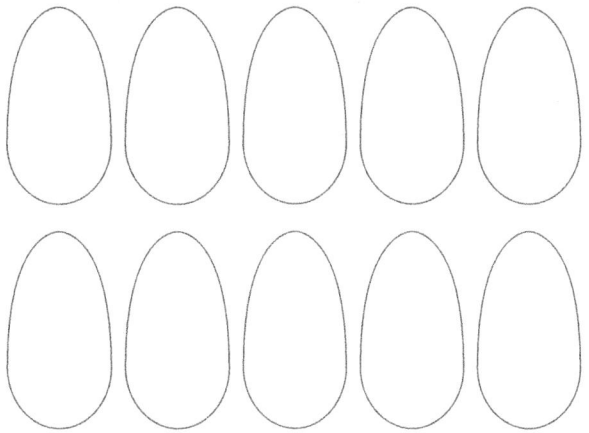

IDEAS / PALETTE

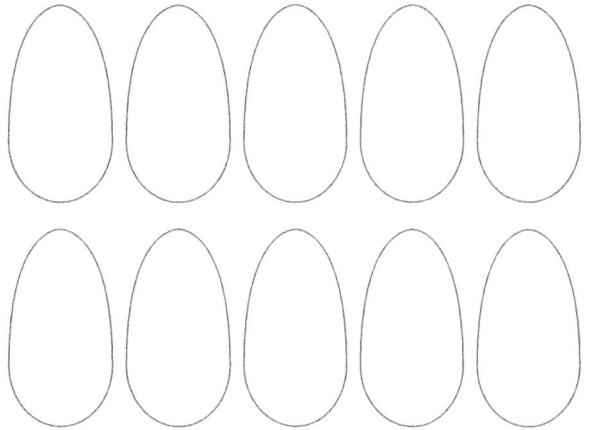

_____

_____

_____

_____

_____

IDEAS / PALETTE

Weekly Prompt

PLAID

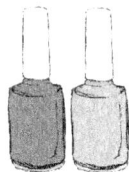

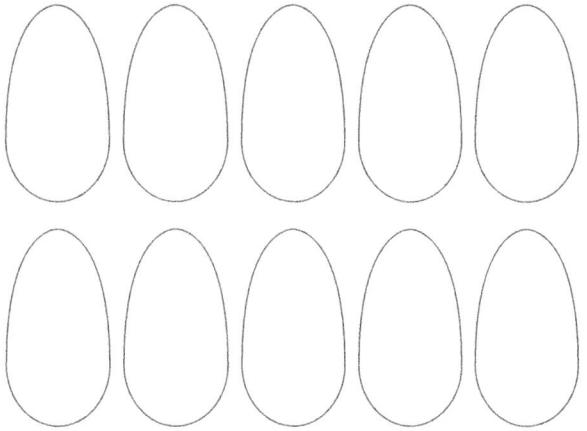

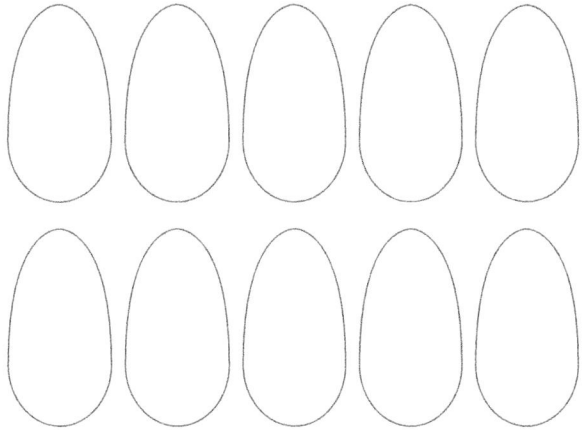

Weekly Prompt

COOKIES

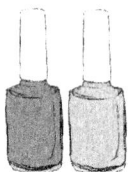

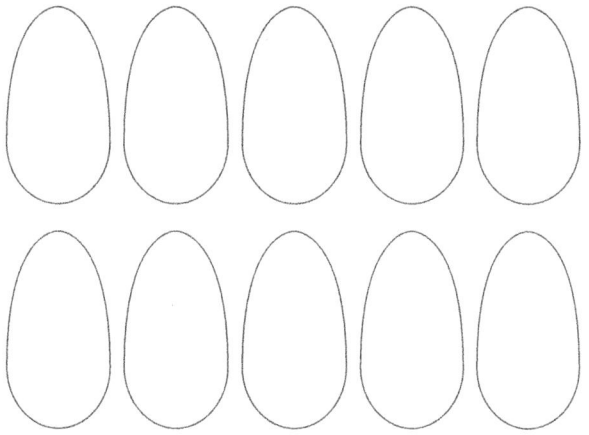

IDEAS / PALETTE

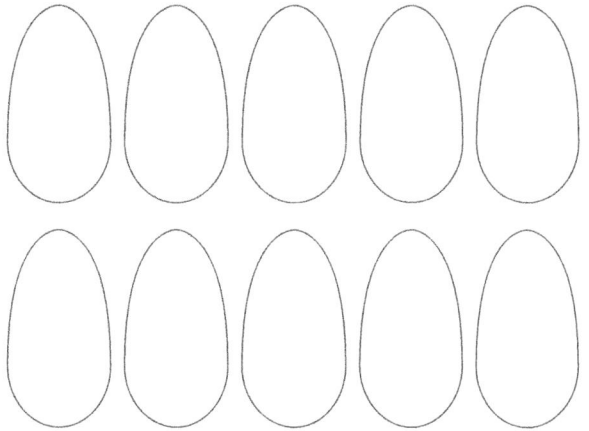

IDEAS / PALETTE

Weekly Prompt

LEAVES

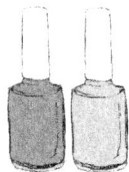

_____
_____
_____
_____
_____
_____

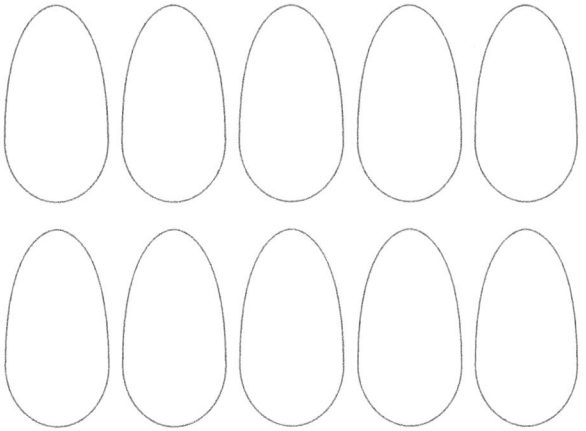

IDEAS / PALETTE

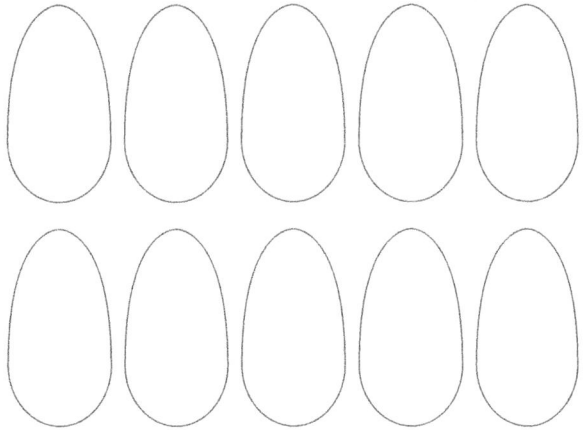

_____
_____
_____
_____
_____

IDEAS / PALETTE

Weekly Prompt

STARS

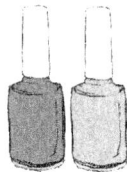

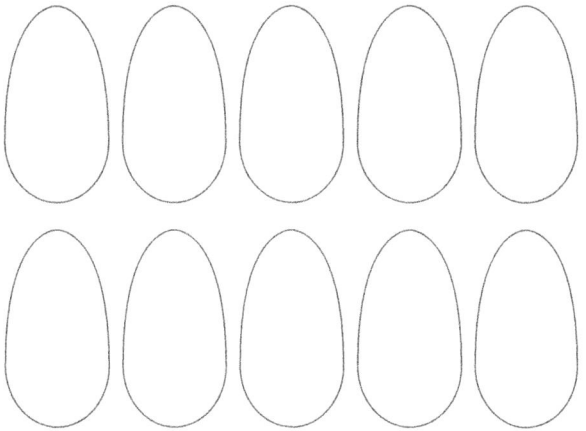

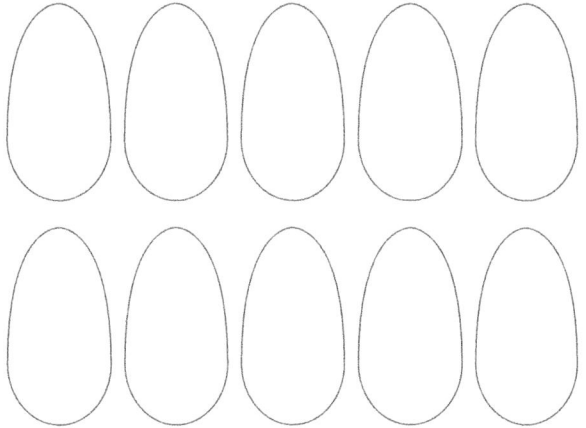

Weekly Prompt

MILK

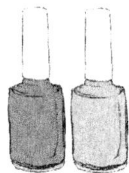

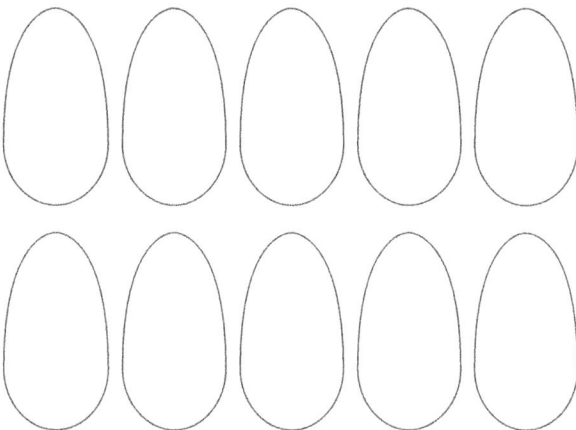

IDEAS / PALETTE

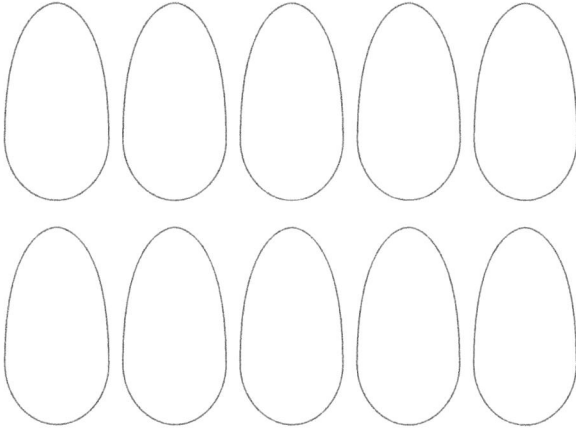

IDEAS / PALETTE

Weekly Prompt

ORNAMENTS

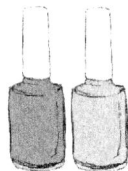

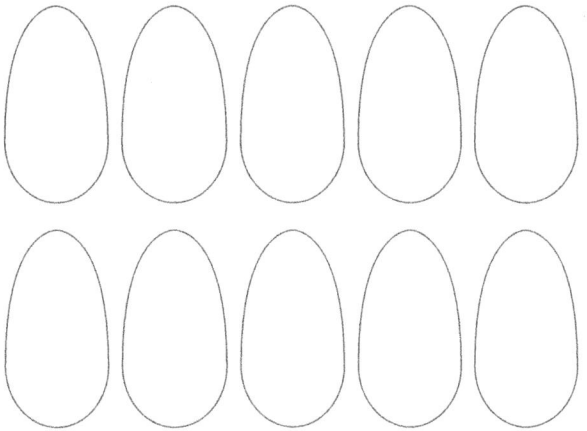

IDEAS / PALETTE

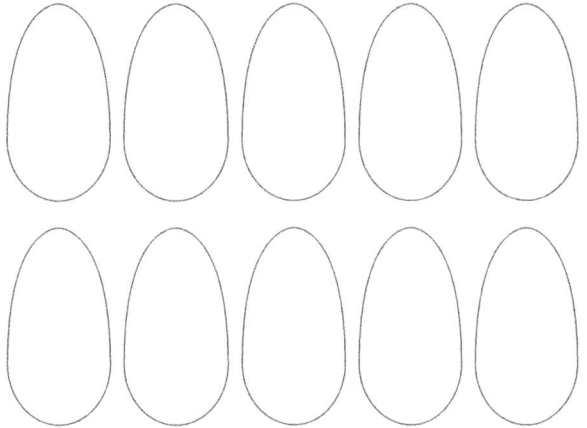

IDEAS / PALETTE

Weekly Prompt

SNOW

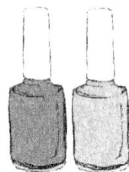

_____

_____

_____

_____

_____

_____

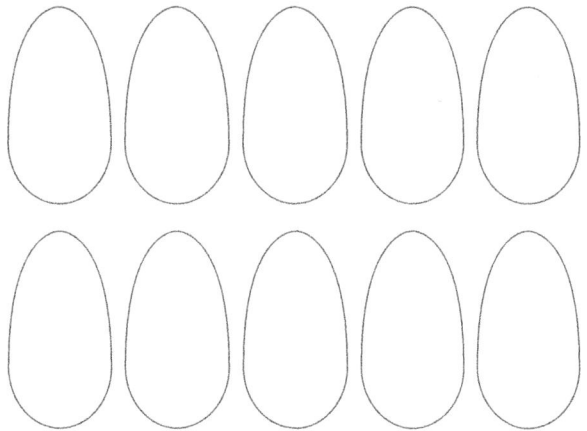

IDEAS / PALETTE

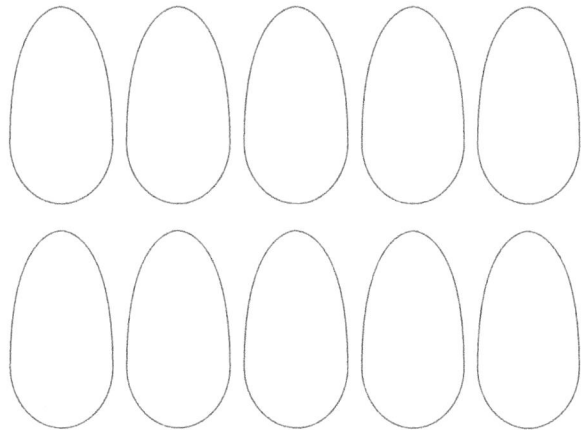

_____

_____

_____

_____

_____

_____

IDEAS / PALETTE

Weekly Prompt

GOLD	FIREWORKS
PIZZA	DOGS
SUNRISE	ICE CREAM
BLUE BIRD	SEA SHELLS
SUSHI	CAMOUFLAGE
HEARTS	ROSES
CHOCOLATE	BACKPACKS
GEOMETRIC SHAPES	SUNSET
CAMERA	WATERMELON
BOOKS	ABSTRACT ART
LUCKY	CATS
STRAWBERRIES	PAISLEY
CHICKENS	COFFEE
PASTEL	SNAKES
UMBRELLAS	FOREST
GALAXY	VAMPIRE
NEGATIVE SPACE	CANDY CORN
MARGARITAS	INK SPLATTER
MERMAIDS	CABLE KNIT
LIGHTNING	PLAID
PINEAPPLES	COOKIES
RAINBOW	LEAVES
BEACH	STARS
PLANETS	MILK
CACTUS	ORNAMENT
OCEAN	SNOW

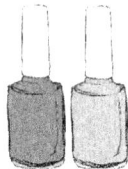

Printed in Great Britain
by Amazon